Be a SUPERHERO in the Kitchen

Donna Glass

illustrated by Alejandro Chamberlain

Menu List

Entrees and Side Dishes

Super Chicken Tacos

Bam! Beef Stew

Eggtastic Spaghetti

Incredible Italian Sausage and Potatoes

Gutsy Garlic Bread Burgers

Zap! Soup in Homemade Bread Bowls

Fearless Chicken and Noodles

Captain Queso Mac

Mega Mac and Cheese Pizza

Reckless Rice Soup

Colossal Bacon and Bean Sidekick

Powerful Potato Cakes

Desserts and Breads

Crime Fighter's Cookie Fluff

Magical Cereal Bars

Legendary Lemon Tarts

Amazing Pudding Parfaits

Awesome Apple Crumble

Boomtastic Butter Cookies

Magnificent Muffin Cones

Beverages

KA-POW! Party Punch

Superhero Cooking Tips

- Always wash your hands before you start cooking!

- Clean your counters before and after you finish making a meal, especially if you have Super Pets. You never know if your Super Friend has walked on the countertop.

- Never cut fruit and vegetables on the same board you cut meat on. Either flip the board over, use two boards, or wash the board between uses.

- You can taste your food as you cook, but never double dip. You don't want your spit to go back into the meal. Never use a finger to taste either. Your hands are dirty from cooking and you don't want to make anyone sick.

- Never eat raw cookie dough. It'll make you sick.

- For slow cooker meals, put a liner in the slow cooker first. It'll make cleanup quick and easy.

- If you don't want to get your hands all icky, wear disposable gloves. That's what all the cool superheroes do anyways.

- Keep a trashcan or trash bowl nearby so you can toss away objects as you go.

- Never put your hand on a hot burner and always use oven mitts when operating an oven. Superheroes take safety seriously!

- Some superheroes have sidekicks to help them in battle. Don't be afraid to ask your kitchen sidekick for help. Remember, fighting crime is like cooking...it takes teamwork!

- Always wash off your raw fruits and vegetables before eating or adding them to a recipe.

**Now that you've read these tips,
go have some fun in the kitchen, Super Chefs!**

Super Chicken Tacos

ingredients

- 3-5 boneless and skinless chicken breasts
- 1 small jar medium chunky style salsa
- 1 small jar salsa con queso
- 6 peppers in a variety of colors
- Taco shells

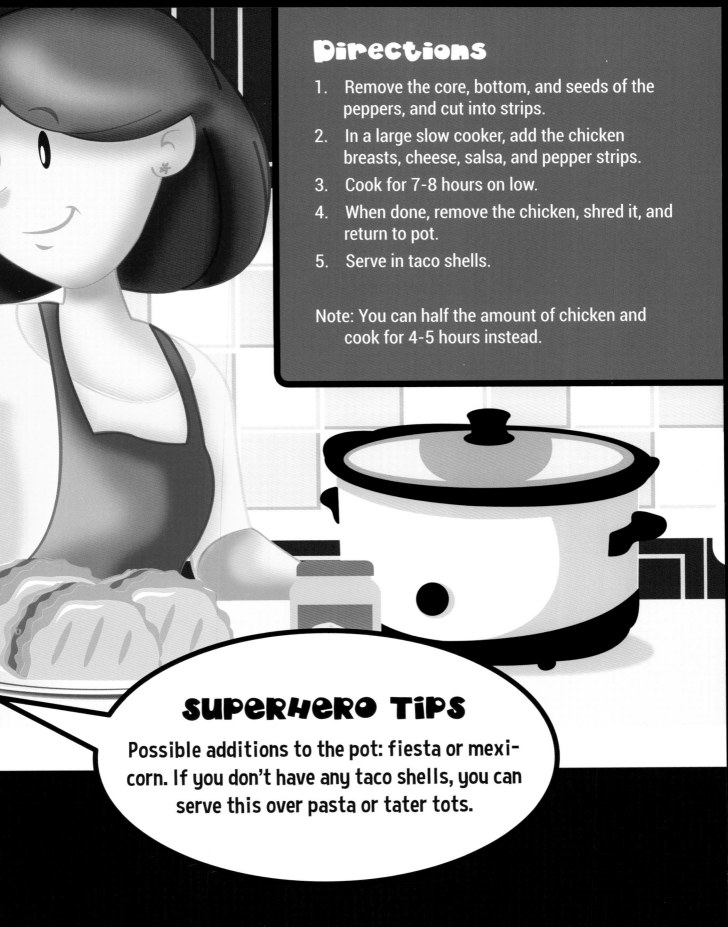

Bam!
Beef Stew

ingredients

- 2 pounds stew meat with the fat trimmed off
- 4 large jars of brown gravy
- 1/2 bag (about 5oz) sliced, matchstick, or diced carrots
- Diced potatoes (dice a couple potatoes or use canned pre-diced potatoes)
- Salt
- Black pepper

Directions

1. Place the stew meat in a large slow cooker and sprinkle with salt and pepper.

2. Add vegetables and gravy to slow cooker. The gravy will thin out in the cooking process. It only looks super thick at first.

3. Cook on low for 8 hours.

4. Serve with bread and/or rice.

Eggtastic Spaghetti

ingredients

- Leftover cooked spaghetti noodles
- 5-6 eggs (2-3 for 1/2 box of cooked noodles)
- 4 tablespoons butter
- Salt
- Black pepper

SUPERHERO TIPS

My family enjoys the spaghetti/egg mixture on waffles with a slice of bacon. I'm not a fan of bacon, so I eat it without. Either way, it's very good.

You don't have to use spaghetti for this recipe. You can use whatever pasta you had from the previous night's dinner. You can also top with crumbled bacon or bacon bits for added protein and to add a bit of texture to the meal.

Directions

1. Melt butter in a pot on the stove over medium heat.
2. Add cooked spaghetti noodles to the pot and stir until the noodles are warmed.
3. Crack eggs over the noodles and add salt and pepper to taste.
4. Stir until eggs cook. They will stick to the noodles and resemble scrambled eggs.

INCREDIBLE Italian Sausage and Potatoes

ingredients

- 1 bag of golden baby potatoes (left whole)
- 2 tablespoons vegetable oil
- 2 beef kielbasa, cut into 1 inch sections
- 1 package of Italian dry seasoning mix
- 1 16-oz jar of deli-sliced peperoncinis
- 1 cup water

Directions

1. Place baby potatoes in a large slow cooker. Drizzle oil over them and toss to coat.
2. Add your sliced kielbasa to the slow cooker.
3. Sprinkle Italian seasoning over it.
4. Pour all the liquid from peperoncini jar over mixture.
5. Top with 1/4 to 1/2 of the peperoncinis left in the jar and 1 cup water.
6. Cook for 7 hours on low.

GUTSY Garlic Bread Burgers

ingredients

- 4 hamburger patties
- 4 sandwich rolls
- Garlic butter
- Your choice of cheese(s)
- Pepperoni (optional)
- Your choice of condiments

Directions

1. Preheat oven to 425°F.

2. Separate tops of sandwich rolls from bottoms and place them on a non-greased cookie sheet facing up. Spread garlic butter and cheese on one or both buns. You can also add the pepperoni if you'd like.

3. Cook for 5-7 minutes in the oven or until cheese is melted.

You can either buy pre-seasoned hamburger patties or make your own. Most stores have hamburger seasoning in the seasoning section.

4. Fry hamburgers on the stove, on an indoor grill, or outside on the grill. Use your digital thermometer to check the temperature of the patties. For a well-done burger, it should read 165°F. Make sure your patties aren't undercooked!

5. Place burgers on the buns and top with your choice of condiments.

6. Serve with fries or chips.

ZAP! SOUP in Homemade Bread Bowls

ingredients

- 1 tube buttermilk biscuits (size large)
- Any soup of your choice
- Cooking spray

Directions

1. Preheat oven to 350°F.
2. Pour soup into a pot and warm on the stove over low to medium heat.
3. Turn 2 (12 count) muffin pans over so openings are now facing down.
4. Spray all sides of the muffin holders.

5. Lay one biscuit over one muffin holder, covering it completely. Repeat with other biscuits, leaving an empty muffin holder between each biscuit. You should be able to make 6 bowls per muffin pan.

6. Bake in oven for 10 minutes or until golden brown.

7. Once done baking, remove pans from the oven. To release the bread bowls, simply flip the pans back over.

8. Ladle soup in each bowl.

FEARLESS Chicken and NOODles

ingredients

- 6 boneless/skinless chicken breasts
- Seasoned salt
- Water
- 4 tablespoons all-purpose flour
- Noodles (short ones like macaroni or rotini work best)

Directions

1. In a pot, add the chicken and sprinkle seasoned salt over it. Cover the chicken completely with water.
2. Cook over medium heat for 2 hours.
3. Once chicken is done, remove it from the pot and shred. Do not discard water.
4. Take a couple cups of the seasoned water and put it in a bowl. Add the flour, cover, and shake well.
5. Add the mixture back to the pot of seasoned water. This will thicken the already seasoned water.
6. Return the shredded chicken to the pot.
7. Simmer on low while you prepare the noodles as directed on package.
8. Drain the noodles in a colander and ladle into a bowl with some chicken and seasoned water.

SUPERHERO TIPS

Make sure to wash your hands and all surfaces after handling raw chicken!

CAPTAIN Queso Mac

SUPERHERO TIPS

Never pour grease down a sink's drain. It will clog your pipes! Try a disposable bowl.

ingredients

- 1 lb lean ground beef
- 1 box shell noodles
- 1 small jar salsa con queso or queso blanco dip
- 1/4 cup milk
- Can of any style corn or a bag of frozen corn

Directions

1. Fill a large pot with water, set on the stove, and turn burner on high heat.

2. While the water is warming up, brown your meat over medium–high heat until no longer pink. Drain off excess grease.

3. Add the cheese and milk to the meat, stir, return to burner, and simmer on low heat.

4. When the water starts to boil, add the noodles and cook according to directions on package.

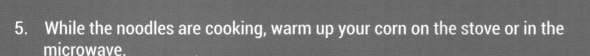

5. While the noodles are cooking, warm up your corn on the stove or in the microwave.

6. After the noodles are cooked, drain them in a colander.

7. On a plate or bowl, ladle a bit of the noodles, meat and cheese mixture, and corn.

8. Serve with garlic bread or nacho chips.

MEGA Mac and Cheese Pizza

Ingredients

- 1 large pre-made pizza crust
- Shredded mozzarella or cheddar cheese
- Any style mac and cheese
- Melted garlic butter
- Black pepper

Directions

1. Prepare your mac and cheese as directed on package.
2. Preheat oven to 450°F.
3. Brush some garlic butter on the crust.

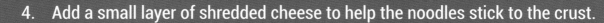

4. Add a small layer of shredded cheese to help the noodles stick to the crust.
5. Spread mac and cheese over the crust.
6. Sprinkle more shredded cheese over the noodles.
7. Add black pepper to taste.
8. Bake for 7-8 minutes or until shredded cheese has melted.

SUPERHERO TIPS

Try adding bacon bits or your favorite pizza toppings!

RECKLESS Rice Soup

ingredients

- 1 cup uncooked long grain rice
- 8 small or 4 large chicken bouillon cubes
- 16 cups water
- 1 yellow onion, diced
- 1/2 cup butter
- Can of diced carrots, drained

Directions

1. Place rice in a medium size pot.
2. Add the water and bouillon cubes.
3. Cook for 30-40 minutes or until the rice puffs up.
4. When the rice is done, remove the pot from heat.
5. Sauté the onion and butter in a small pan. Once the onions are tender, add it to the pot of rice along with carrots.
6. Let the mixture sit for 5-10 minutes to allow time for the carrots to cook in the hot broth.

COLOSSAL Bacon and Bean-Sidekick

ingredients

- 1-1/2 pounds green beans, washed and trimmed
- 1 can of sweet corn, drained
- 3 strips original-style bacon
- 2 tablespoons butter
- 1 cup water
- Sea salt
- Black pepper

Directions

1. Preheat oven to 400°F.
2. Place bacon on cookie sheet and cook for about 18 minutes or until crispy.
3. Wash the green beans, snapping off ends.

4. Place a large skillet over high heat. Add the green beans, corn, and water. Bring to a boil, cover, and cook 3-4 minutes.

5. Remove lid, add butter and seasoning. Cook for an additional 3-5 minutes or until butter melts and water has fully evaporated. Remove from heat.

6. When the bacon is done, remove it from the cookie sheets using tongs, patting off excess grease. Wait a couple minutes for bacon to cool and then break into pieces to sprinkle over vegetables.

7. Stir and serve with a protein (chicken, fish, or meat).

POWERFUL Potato Cakes

This recipe calls for hot oil! Hot oil can be very dangerous, so please never leave the oil or your child unattended!

ingredients

- 10 russet potatoes, peeled and grated
- 1/2 yellow onion, peeled and grated
- 1 egg
- 1 cup flour
- Salt
- Vegetable oil

SUPERHERO TIPS

For easy flipping, use two spatulas, one under the potato cake and one on top.

You can serve these with sausage, steak, fried eggs, or whatever protein is handy.

Directions

1. Heat a 12-inch skillet over low-medium heat.
2. Next, add enough oil to reach 1/2 inch in depth. You'll know when the oil is hot enough when you add a drop of water and it sizzles at the surface.
3. In a large bowl, stir together the grated potatoes, grated onion, egg, flour, and salt.
4. Carefully spoon about a 1/4 - 1/2 cup of the potato mixture onto the oil.
5. When you notice the corner edges browning, carefully flip the cake over.
6. After both sides are brown and crispy, remove and place on a plate covered in paper towels. The towels will help soak up the excess oil.

CRIME FIGHTER'S Cookie Fluff

ingredients

- 1 large box or 2 small boxes of vanilla pudding mixes
- Milk
- 1 tub of whipped topping (sugar free)
- 1 box of chocolate chip cookies, broken into pieces

Directions

1. Make pudding according to directions on the package.
2. Let set in fridge for 10-15 minutes.
3. Stir in whipped topping and cookies.
4. Chill for a few hours. The longer it sits in the refrigerator, the softer the cookies will get.

SUPERHERO TIPS

You can use skim milk in the pudding to cut calories, but whole milk or 2% works just as good.

Experiment with different cookies and pudding! Strawberry cream pudding and vanilla wafers? Cookies and cream pudding with mini sandwich cookies? Try them out!

MAGICAL Cereal Bars

ingredients

- 1 bag multicolored and flavored marshmallows
- 1 box rainbow cereal
- 3 tablespoons butter

Directions

1. Melt butter on low in a large pot.
2. Stir in marshmallows. Keep stirring until melted.
3. Add 3/4 bag of rainbow cereal. Stir to coat the cereal.
4. Cover a 13x9 cake pan with parchment paper and spray with cooking spray.
5. Press the cereal mixture onto the pan and let cool.
6. Once cool, cut into squares and serve.

LEGENDARY
Lemon Tarts

ingredients

- 1 tube of crescent rolls
- Small jar of lemon fruit filling
- 3/4 cup powdered sugar
- 1-1/2 tablespoons milk
- 1/4 teaspoon lemon extract

Directions

1. Preheat oven to 350°F.
2. Spray large cooking sheet with cooking spray.
3. Open crescent roll tube and unroll onto cookie sheet. Separate into four sections of two crescent rolls still attached together.
4. Starting with the first section, press together the perforated lines connecting the crescent rolls. Repeat on other three sections.

5. Spread a thin layer of lemon filling over each roll. Take one end, pull toward the other side, and press edges to seal. Pinch closed any other gaps you find. Repeat for each roll.

6. Bake 9 minutes or until golden brown.

7. Mix powdered sugar, milk, and lemon extract together in a small bowl.

8. Drizzle the glaze over the tarts and serve while warm.

AMAZING PUDDING PARFAITS

ingredients

- 1 (3.4 oz.) box strawberry pudding dry mix
- 1 (3.4 oz.) box vanilla pudding dry mix
- 1 (3.4 oz.) box chocolate pudding dry mix
- Skim milk (6 cups, 2 cups per mix)
- Whipped topping

Directions

1. Make each pudding according to their instructions. Keep each one in their very own bowl.

2. Put puddings in the refrigerator until set, about 15 minutes.

3. Once they've set, take parfait glasses and begin layering the puddings. It doesn't matter if you start with strawberry as the bottom layer or chocolate. However, I always put vanilla in the middle.

4. After the three layers are in the glasses, spread some whipped topping over it.

SUPERHERO TIPS

Try sliced strawberries or chocolate sprinkles as a topping!

AWESOME APPLE CRUMBLE

ingredients

- 2 cans apple pie filling
- 1-1/2 – 2 teaspoons ground cinnamon
- 1-1/3 cup graham cracker crumbs
- 1/3 cup butter or margarine, melted
- Cooking spray

SUPERHERO TIPS

Don't be afraid to taste test your apple filling first! Not enough cinnamon for you? Add some more!

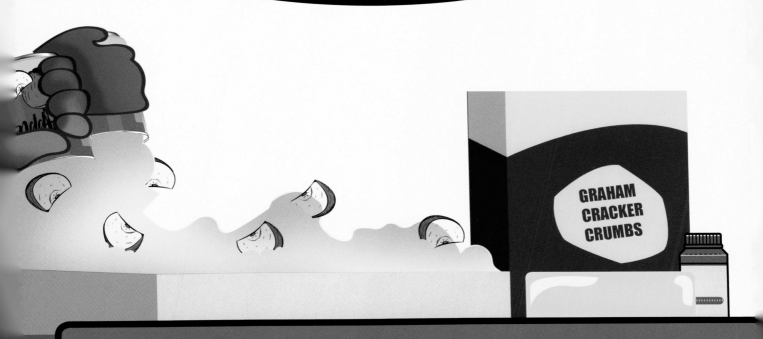

Directions

1. Preheat oven to 375° F.

2. Coat an 8x8 aluminum baking pan with cooking spray.

3. Pour the apple pie filling into the pan. Use the side of a spoon to cut the apple pieces into smaller chunks.

4. Sprinkle cinnamon over apples, stirring well. The mixture will become dark brown.

5. In a bowl, mix graham cracker crumbs and melted butter. Spoon over pie filling.

6. Bake for 20 minutes or until dark brown.

7. Cool about 10 minutes and then serve with ice cream or whipped topping.

BOOMTASTIC Butter Cookies

SUPERHERO TIPS

The dough is sticky, so you may need to scrape the sides of the bowl when mixing.

ingredients

- 1 cup unsalted butter, softened
- 1/2 cup cane sugar blend
- 2 extra-large eggs
- 2 tsp. vanilla extract
- 2-1/2 cups flour, plus extra for rolling
- 2 tsp. baking powder
- Couple pinches *of salt*
- Powdered sugar

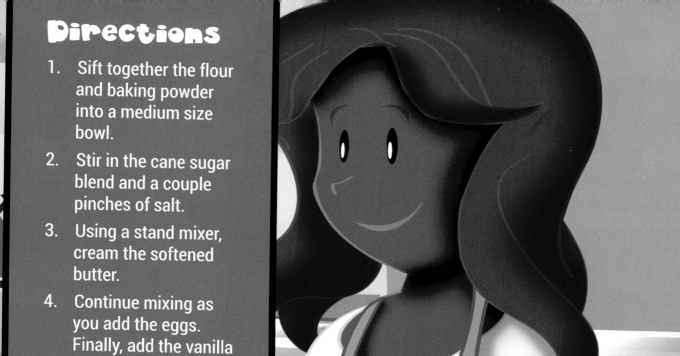

Directions

1. Sift together the flour and baking powder into a medium size bowl.

2. Stir in the cane sugar blend and a couple pinches of salt.

3. Using a stand mixer, cream the softened butter.

4. Continue mixing as you add the eggs. Finally, add the vanilla extract.

5. Slowly scoop the dry ingredients into the mixer.

6. Once a dough has formed, cover and chill in refrigerator for 30 minutes.

7. Preheat the oven to 350°F and generously dust your countertop and rolling pin with flour.

8. Remove the sticky dough from the bowl and roll out flat, about 1/8 inch thick. Use tiny cookie cutters to create shapes.

9. Place shapes onto a greased cookie sheet and bake for about 10 minutes or until bottoms have browned.

10. Move warm cookies to a wire rack and dust with powdered sugar.

MAGNIFICENT Muffin cones

ingredients

- 1 box of muffin mix (that makes 6 per package)
- Skim milk
- 10 flat bottom ice cream cones

SUPERHERO TIPS

If you ice them while the muffins are hot, eat right away or the icing will melt!

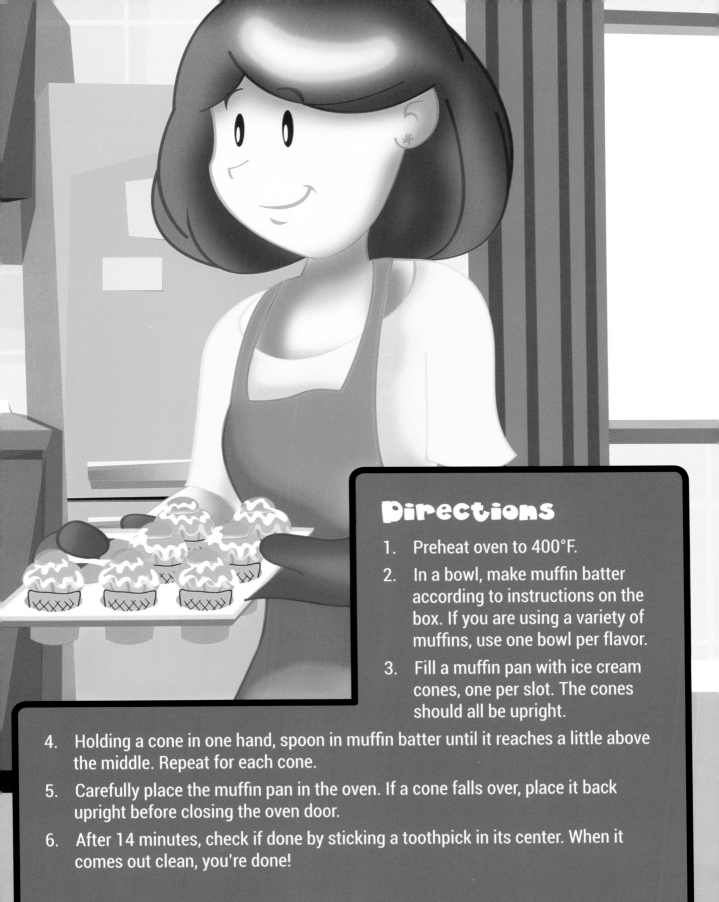

Directions

1. Preheat oven to 400°F.

2. In a bowl, make muffin batter according to instructions on the box. If you are using a variety of muffins, use one bowl per flavor.

3. Fill a muffin pan with ice cream cones, one per slot. The cones should all be upright.

4. Holding a cone in one hand, spoon in muffin batter until it reaches a little above the middle. Repeat for each cone.

5. Carefully place the muffin pan in the oven. If a cone falls over, place it back upright before closing the oven door.

6. After 14 minutes, check if done by sticking a toothpick in its center. When it comes out clean, you're done!

KA-POW! Party Punch

ingredients

- 1 gallon red fruit punch
- 2 liter bottle of grapefruit-citrus soda
- 1 quart vanilla ice cream

Directions

1. Put ice cream into large punch bowl and then add equal amounts of soda and fruit punch.

2. Serve with a ladle.

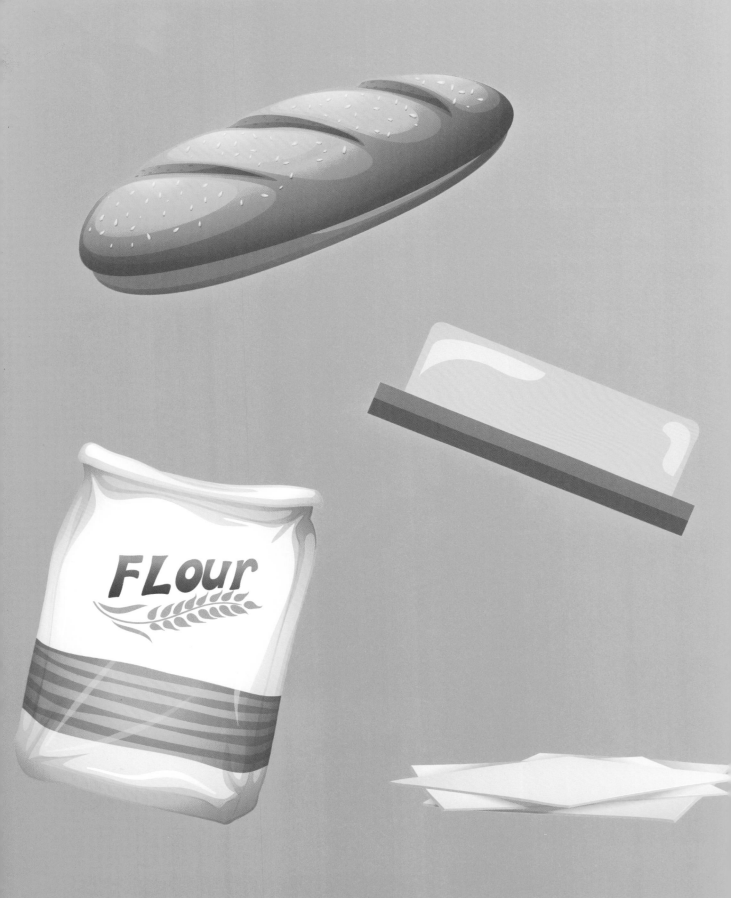